ANIMALS AND THEIR BABIES

Ducks and Ducklings

written by Anita Ganeri

illustrated by Anni Axworthy

A+

Smart Apple Media

This book has been published in cooperation with Evans Publishing Group.

Copyright © Evans Brothers Limited 2007
Text Copyright © Anita Ganeri 2007
Illustrations Copyright © Anni Axworthy
This edition published under license from Evans Brothers Limited
All right reserved

Published in the United States by Smart Apple Media
2140 Howard Drive West, North Mankato, Minnesota 56003

Library of Congress Cataloging-in-Publication Data

Ganeri, Anita, 1961-
Ducks and ducklings / by Anita Ganeri.
p.cm. - (Animals and their babies)
Includes index.
ISBN 978-1-58340-810-0
1. Ducklings—Juvenile literature. 2. Ducks—Juvenile literature. I. Title.

QL696.A52G345 2007
598.4'1139—dc22   2006103530

9 8 7 6 5 4 3 2 1

CONTENTS

A duck starts life inside an egg. In spring, the female duck lays her eggs beside a pond. She makes a nest from grass and leaves. She puts warm, fluffy feathers in it.

The female lays an egg every day or two until there are about 12 eggs. The male duck chases other ducks away so that they do not harm the eggs. Then he swims away.

The mother duck sits on the eggs to keep them warm. This helps the baby ducks grow inside the eggs. The mother duck only gets up to find food and stretch her legs.

Animals such as foxes like to eat duck eggs. The mother duck's speckled, brown feathers match the color of the ground. This helps hide the mother duck and the nest.

9

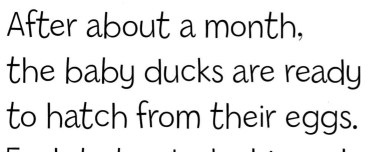

After about a month,
the baby ducks are ready
to hatch from their eggs.
Each baby duck chips a hole in
the eggshell with its sharp little beak.

Baby ducks are called ducklings. They are covered in soft, fluffy feathers called down. They chirp as they come out of their eggs.

The new ducklings are very hungry.
About 12 hours after hatching from
their eggs, they are ready to leave
their nest to find food.

Their mother leads the ducklings to the pond
for their first swim. They have webbed feet
for paddling through the water. They swim close
to their mother.

The mother duck shows the ducklings what they can eat. They eat seeds and water plants, snails, insects, and shellfish.

The ducklings scoop some of their food from the surface of the water. They also reach under the water to find plants to eat.

Young ducklings are sometimes eaten by fish and birds. If the mother duck sees danger, she quacks loudly so that the ducklings come to her.

At night, the ducklings snuggle under their mother's wings. This helps keep them safe and warm if the weather is cold.

When the ducklings are about two months old, they are ready to learn to fly.

First, they have to practice flapping their wings.

18

Ducks are fast, strong fliers. They fly with other ducks in big groups called flocks. They flap their wings to take off from the water and spread their wings to land.

The duckling is a year old.
It is now a grown-up duck.

A male duck usually has brightly
colored feathers. A female duck
has plain brown feathers.

The duck is old enough to have its own ducklings. In fall, a male and female duck meet. Next spring, the female duck lays her eggs. The eggs hatch into . . . new ducklings!

Index

Further Information

The ducks featured in this book are mallards (*Anas platyrhynchus*). To find out more about them, you can visit: www.nhptv.org/Natureworks/mallard.htm, the NatureWorks Web site sponsored by New Hampshire Public Television.